JOKE BOOK
CHRISTMAS
EDITION

Welcome to our Joke Book,
a delightful collection of laughs
for the whole family!
Start your journey with festive
Christmas jokes to bring extra
cheer to your holidays.
Continue chuckling with jokes
about **sports, food, animals,
vacations, school, and so
much more**. Perfect for kids,
teens, and adults alike, this book
is your go-to source for fun and
laughter anytime, anywhere.

What kind of cars do elves drive?

Toy-otas!

Why did Santa get a parking ticket on Christmas Eve?

He left his sleigh in a snow-parking zone!

What do reindeer hang on their Christmas trees?

Hornaments!

DAY 1

Why don't Christmas trees knit?

They always drop
their needles!

What does a Christmas tree say when it stands up too fast?

I'm feeling a little
light-headed!

Why was the Christmas sweater so bad at telling jokes?

Because it was a
real knitwit!

What kind of car does a sheep drive?

A lamborghini!

Why don't ships ever get lonely?

Because they're always surrounded by their buoys!

What's a car's favorite meal?

Brake-fast!

What runs but doesn't get anywhere?

A refrigerator!

Why do bees have sticky hair?

Because they use honeycombs!

What did the buffalo say when his son left for college?

Bison!

DAY 2

What's a Christmas tree's favorite candy?

Orna-mints!

What did one snowflake say to the other?

You're one of a kind!

Why did the gingerbread man go to therapy?

He was feeling crumby.

DAY 2

Why don't you ever see Santa in the hospital?

Because he has private elf care!

Why was the snowman looking through the carrots?

He was picking his nose!

Why did the Christmas tree go to the barber?

It needed to trim its branches!

Why did the cow go to outer space?

To visit the Milky Way!

What do you call a bear that's stuck in the rain?

A drizzly bear!

Why did the turtle cross the road?

To get to the shell station!

Why did the mom put the clock in the oven?

Because she wanted time to cook!

Why did the dad bring a ladder to the family dinner?

Because he wanted to reach new heights!

Why did the kid bring a spoon to bed?

Because he wanted a little scoop of sleep!

What do you get when you cross a pig and a Christmas tree?

A porcupine.

I bought my Dad a cheap dictionary for Christmas. He couldn't find the right words to thank me.

How much did Santa pay for his sleigh?

Nothing, it was on the house!

DAY 3

What do you call a reindeer who tells jokes?

A stand-up comedi-deer!

Christmas lights remind me of my friends. They all hang together, half of them don't work, and the ones that do aren't that bright.

What did the bald man say when he got a comb for Christmas?

'Thanks, I'll never part with it.'

What do you get when you cross a snake and a pie?

A pie-thon!

Why don't ostriches ever become pilots?

Because they always stick their heads in the ground!

What do you call a penguin in the desert?

Lost!

Why did the suitcase go to therapy?

Because it couldn't handle the baggage!

Where do pencils go on vacation?

To Pennsylvania!

What did the ocean say to the beach?

Nothing, it just waved!

What did the bald man say when he got a comb for Christmas?
'Thanks, I'll never part with it.'

What is the linguistic description of sentences like 'ho ho ho' and 'merry Christmas'?

They are both Santa clauses.

What did the banker get for Christmas?
My 401k.

I got the most classic, timeless Christmas present this year.

A broken watch.

What does Father Christmas call that reindeer with no eyes?

No-eyed-deer!

What did a crab say to another crab on Christmas?

Hey, Sandy Claws.

DAY 4

Where do cows go on vacation?

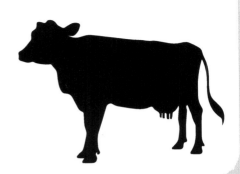

Moo York!

Why don't skeletons ever go on vacation?

Because they have no body to go with!

What do you call a snowman on vacation?

A puddle!

How does the moon cut his hair?

Eclipse it!

Why did the invisible man turn down the job offer?

He couldn't see himself doing it!

What do you call a belt made of watches?

A waist of time!

What's Scrooge's favorite Christmas game?

Mean-opoly.

What do you give a train driver for Christmas?

Platform shoes!

This year for Christmas, I asked for a new pair of scissors...

My old pair just wasn't cutting it!

What kind of cards do donkeys send out near Christmas?

Mule-tide greetings.

Why does Father Christmas like to work in the garden?

Because he likes to hoe hoe hoe.

What's Tarzan's favorite Christmas song?

Jungle Bells.

Where do sheep go on vacation?

To the baa-hamas!

What travels around the world but stays in one corner?

A stamp!

What did one volcano say to the other on vacation?

I lava you!

Why did the washing machine break up with the dryer?

Because it felt agitated!

Why do carpets never get lost?

Because they always know where to lay down!

Why did the vacuum cleaner apply for a job?

Because it really sucked at everything else!

What did one Christmas tree say to the other?

Lighten up!

Did you hear about the Power Plant that was bad for the environment all year?

He got coal for Christmas.

What does Ebenezer Scrooge serve at his Christmas party?

Humburgers!

DAY 6

What is Father Christmas's tax status?

Elf-employed.

Where do snowmen go to dance?

The snowball!

Who brings the Christmas presents to police stations?

Santa Clues.

What did the bug say to the windshield?

"You're really bugging me!"

Why don't spiders ever leave home?

Because they're always caught up in their webs!

What do you call a bug that lives at the gym?

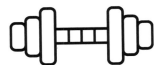

A dumb-bug!

What time is it when the clock strikes 13?

Time to get a new clock!

What did the zero say to the eight?

0 8

Nice belt!

What did one wall say to the other wall?

I'll meet you at the corner!

DAY 7

What do ducks do at Christmas time?
They duckerate cookies.

What did the ghosts say to Santa Claus?
We'll have a boo Christmas without you.

Last week, I told my grandpa that Amazon is the best place for Christmas shopping.
He just called me from Brazil.

What did Dracula say at the Christmas party?

Fancy a bite.

This year I've decided I'm going to exercise religiously...

That means I'm going to work out on Easter and Christmas, and I'm done.

What types of trees never get Christmas presents?

Knotty Pines.

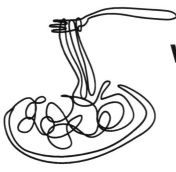

What do you call fake spaghetti?

An impasta!

How does a cucumber become a pickle?

It goes through a jarring experience!

What kind of cheese is made backward?

Edam!

DAY 7

Why was the teacher wearing sunglasses in the classroom?

Because her students were so bright!

Why don't scientists trust atoms?

Because they make up everything!

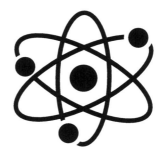

Why did the student bring a ladder to school?

Because she wanted to go to high school!

DAY 8

What is a dog's favorite Christmas song?

Fleas Navidad.

How do sheep greet each other at Christmas?

A merry Christmas to ewe.

What did Adam say on the day before Christmas?

It's Christmas, Eve!

DAY 8

What's the best gift you can buy at Christmas?

A broken drum, you can't beat it.

What did the snowman say when he got coal for Christmas?

"I can see!"

Why don't reindeer play board games?

Because they always hoof around the rules!

Why did the scarecrow win an award?

Because he was outstanding in his field!

What do you call an owl that does magic tricks?

Hooo-dini!

Why are fish bad at basketball?

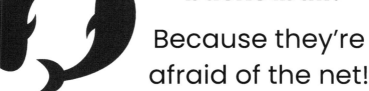

Because they're afraid of the net!

DAY 8

Why can't a nose be 12 inches long?

Because then it would be a foot!

Why don't programmers like nature?

It has too many bugs!

Why did the kid throw a clock out the window?

He wanted to see time fly!

Why do snowmen love winter?

It's the only time they can chill!

What is a snowman's favorite drink?

Iced tea!

What did Jack Frost say to the snowman?

Have an ice day!

What's the best part about building a snowman?

It's snow much fun!

Why do snowmen never get into arguments?

Because they just let things melt away!

Why did the snowman stay home from the party?

Because he had snow-one to go with!

Why did the chicken join a band?

Because it had the drumsticks!

What do you get when you cross a bear with a skunk?

Winnie the P-U!

Why are cats good at video games?

Because they have nine lives!

Why was the math book always sad?

Because it had too many problems!

Why did the student eat his homework?

Because the teacher said it was a piece of cake!

Why did the pencil go to the principal's office?

Because it was caught being sharp!

How does
Jack Frost
get to work?

By icicles.

What is the difference
between the Christmas
alphabet and the
ordinary alphabet?

The Christmas alphabet
has NO EL.

Did you hear about the
man who stole the
advent calendar?

He got 25 days.

DAY 10

What do you call a reindeer with bad manners?

Rude-olph!

Why don't penguins like talking to strangers?

They find it hard to break the ice!

What did the one hat say to the other?

Stay here, I'm going on ahead!

What do you call a boomerang that doesn't come back?

A stick!

What did one elevator say to the other?

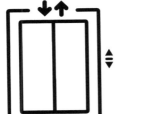 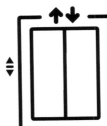

I think I'm coming down with something!

Why did the math teacher write on the window?

Because he wanted his lesson to be clear!

What do you call two birds in love?

Tweethearts!

What did the rabbit say to his girlfriend?

Somebunny loves you!

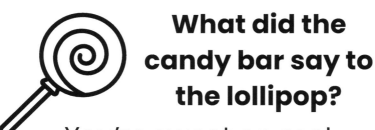

What did the candy bar say to the lollipop?

You're sweet on me!

What does a snowman like to eat for lunch?

Icebergers!

Why did the skier bring a pencil to the slopes?

He wanted to draw some attention!

Why did the snowman's computer keep freezing?

It left too many windows open!

How did Darth Vader know what Luke got him for Christmas?

He felt his presents.

At work, I noticed the computer department has started putting Christmas decorations up.

IT's beginning to look a lot like Christmas.

Last year's Christmas pudding was so awful I threw it in the ocean.

That's probably why the ocean's full of currants!

Why did the cow go to space?

To see the mooo-n!

What's a cat's favorite color?

Purr-ple!

Why don't dogs make good dancers?

Because they have two left feet!

Why did the staircase complain?

Because it was always being stepped on!

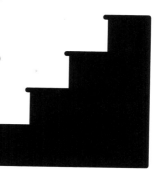

Why do beds never tell secrets?

Because they don't want to spread rumors!

Why don't toasters ever tell jokes?

Because they always get a burnt reaction!

What did the strawberry say on December 25th?

Berry Christmas!

What falls in winter but never gets hurt?

Snow!

What does Father Christmas suffer from if he gets stuck in a chimney?

Santa Claustrophobia!

What did one Christmas light say to the other?

You light up my life!

How do Christmas trees get ready for a night out?

They put on their lights!

Why did the Christmas lights break up?

They just couldn't keep it together anymore!

DAY 12

What did the couch say when it was invited to the party?

I'm too tired, I'll just lounge around!

Why did the calendar feel so stressed out?

Because its days were numbered!

Why don't books ever get cold?

Because they have covers!

Why don't ants get sick?

Because they have tiny ant-bodies!

Why do gorillas have big nostrils?

Because they have big fingers!

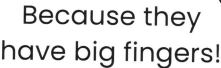

Why did the bird go to the hospital?

It needed tweetment!

Why didn't the Christmas Cake go to the dance?

He had his raisins.

What do you call a line of men waiting for a haircut?

A barbecue.

What's the best thing to bring to your holiday party?

A Christmas tree. Because they're lit.

What do you call an Elf that sings?

A wrapper!

What does Father Christmas call his money?

Iced lolly.

What do you get when you cross an apple with a Christmas tree?

A pear.

What's a caterpillar's favorite sport?

Rugby—because it's always a scrum!

Why did the spider go to the computer?

To check its web-site!

What do you get if you cross a centipede with a parrot?

A walkie-talkie!

Why did the microwave get a job?

Because it wanted to make hot money!

Why did the picture go to jail?
Because it was framed!

What's the best part of living in a smart house?

The walls always have something to say!

Did you hear about Dracula's Christmas party?

It was a scream!

What's the best thing to put into a Christmas cake?

Your teeth!

Why is a cat on a beach like Christmas?

Because they both have "Sandy claws"!

How does NASA organize their Christmas party?

They planet.

What song do Father Christmas' gnomes sing to him when he comes home cold on Christmas night?

Freeze a jolly good fellow!

What are you getting this Christmas?

Fatter.

Why are frogs so happy?

Because they eat whatever bugs them!

What kind of dog loves to take baths?

A shampoo-dle!

Why did the owl say "Hoo's there?"

Because it was an owl knock-knock joke!

Why don't roofs ever get lonely?

Because they're always on top of things!

What kind of room has no doors or windows?

A mushroom!

Why do lamps make good friends?

Because they always brighten your day!

All I got for Christmas was a pack of sticky cards. It was difficult to deal with.

What song do you sing if you're not a fan of Christmas?

Sigh-lent night.

What will fall on the lawn first?

An autumn leaf or a Christmas catalog?

How many chimneys does Father Christmas go down?

Stacks!

I asked for a new gaming console for Christmas, instead I got some torn-up cardboard. I asked why.

"I thought you asked for an ex-box!"

What did the bad soccer announcer get for Christmas?

COOOOOOOOOO AAAAAAAALLLLLLLLLLLLLL LLLLL!!!!!!!!!!!!!!!!!!!!!!!

What do you call a potato wearing glasses?

A spectator!

Why don't oranges ever exercise?

Because they're always getting juiced!

Why did the banana go to the doctor?

Because it wasn't peeling very well!

What's a mosquito's favorite sport?

Skin diving!

Why was the caterpillar always on the phone?

Because it was making butterfly calls!

What did the grasshopper say to the bug?

You're really hopping on my nerves!

What do elves use to take selfies?

An "elfie" stick!

It was Christmastime, and everybody was feeling Merry.
So she went home.

What will Tesla build this Christmas to help Santa deliver presents?
An elf-driving car.

What did the TV get for Christmas?

Replaced.

Father Christmas: I like the story about the girl who steals from the rich and gives it all to Granny.

Elf: That's Little Red Robin Hood!

What did Pinocchio say to Rudolph when he asked him what he wanted for Christmas?

Quit being nosey.

Why do fish live in salt water?

Because pepper makes them sneeze!

What do you call a dog magician?

A labracadabrador!

Why did the leopard wear a disguise?

Because he didn't want to be spotted!

Why don't kangaroos ever get lost?

Because they always keep bouncing back!

What do you call a sleeping dinosaur?

A dino-snore!

Why don't elephants chew gum?

Because they're afraid of popping it!

What's different about an American Christmas from a Spanish one?
Noel.

Christmas with the family:

While I greatly enjoy the presence of their company, I prefer the company of their presents.

My daughter asked for Frozen stuff for Christmas, so I bought her frozen chips and a packet of peas.

Why did the Christmas tree go to therapy?

It had too many hang-ups!

Why was E the only letter in the alphabet to get Christmas presents?

Because the rest of the letters are not-E.

Who's there?

Centipede. Centipede who? Centipede under the Christmas tree.

Why did the coffee file a police report?

Because it got mugged!

What kind of room doesn't have doors?

A mushroom!

Why don't we tell secrets in a cornfield?

Because the corn has ears!

What did one firefly say to the other?

You light up my life!

Why are spiders great baseball players?

Because they know how to catch flies!

What do you call a snail on a ship?

A snailor!

Why is it so cold at Christmas?
It's in Decembrrrrr.

How do you scare a snowman?

You get a hair-dryer!

What do you get when you combine a Christmas tree with an iPad?

A pineapple.

DAY 18

Why don't mountains ever get cold in the winter?

They wear snowcaps!

Why didn't the skeleton go snowboarding?

He didn't have the guts!

What do you call an old snowman?
Water!

How do you organize a space party?

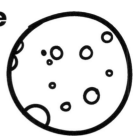

You planet!

Why did the cookie cry?

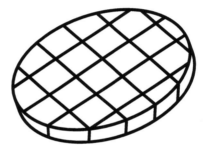

Because his mother was a wafer so long!

Why did the tree go to the dentist?

It needed a root canal!

Why did the frog take the bus to work?

Because his car got toad!

Why did the physics teacher break up with the biology teacher?

There was no chemistry.

Why did the man name his dogs Rolex and Timex?

Because they were watchdogs!

Why don't soccer players wear glasses?

Because it's a contact sport!

Why can't pigs play soccer?

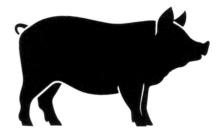

They always keep the ball for themselves.

What does a sprinter eat before a race?

Nothing, they're fasting!

I used to be obsessed with basketball, but I've bounced back.

Why don't fish play basketball?

They're scared of the net.

Why shouldn't you play tennis in the jungle?

There are too many cheetahs.

What's a vegetable's favorite type of joke?
A corny one!

Why did the mushroom go to the party?
Because he was a fungi!

What did the baby corn say to the mama corn?
Where's popcorn?

What do you get when you cross a cow and a duck?

Milk and quackers!

Why do crabs never share?

Because they're shellfish!

What's a snake's favorite subject in school?

Hiss-tory!

Why don't soccer players wear glasses?

Because it's a contact sport!

What's the best animal in soccer?

A score-pion!

Why couldn't the baby score in basketball?

He was too busy drooling on the ball.

Why did the baseball player get fired?

He ran to third base, then walked home.

Where do basketball players get their uniforms?

From New Jersey.

Why do fathers take an extra pair of socks when they go golfing?

Just in case they score a hole-in-one!

What do you get when you cross a sheep and a kangaroo?

 A woolly jumper!

Why do cows wear bells?

Because their horns don't work!

What do you get when you cross a cow and a trampoline?

A milkshake!

Why did the broom get a promotion?
Because it swept the competition!

Why don't you ever fight with a pillow?

Because it's always too soft!

Why did the door go to school?

To learn how to get a handle on things!

Why don't basketball players ever go on vacation?

They'd get called for traveling!

What's the difference between a baby and a quarterback?

One takes naps, the other takes snaps.

Why did the tennis player bring a ladder to the court?

To reach new heights!

Why can't football players ever tell secrets?

Because they're always wide open!

Why did the bicycle fall over?

Because it was two-tired!

What do you call a pig who plays basketball?

A real ball hog!

What do you call an elephant that doesn't matter?

An irrelephant!

Why don't crocodiles like fast food?

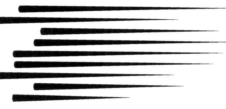

Because they can't catch it!

What kind of key opens a banana?

A monKEY!

What did one plate say to the other?

Lunch is on me!

What's the strongest vegetable?

A muscle sprout!

What do you call a sad strawberry?

A blueberry!

What kind of shoes do bakers wear?
Loafers!

Why did the tomato turn red?
Because it saw the salad dressing!

I would tell you a joke about pizza, but it's too cheesy.

Why don't bananas ever get lonely?
Because they hang out in bunches!

What did the lettuce say to the celery?
Quit stalking me!

How do you fix a broken pizza?
With tomato paste!

Why did the computer go to the doctor?

Because it had a virus!

What did the left eye say to the right eye?

Between us, something smells!

What did the traffic light say to the car?

Don't look, I'm changing!

Why did the orange stop halfway up the hill?
Because it ran
out of juice!

What do you call cheese that isn't yours?
Nacho cheese!

How do you make a lemon drop?

Just let it fall!

DAY 23

Why are oranges the smartest fruit?

Because they're made of concentrate!

What did the butter say to the bread?

I'm on a roll!

Why did the butter bring a towel?

Because it was going to butter up!

Why did the phone break up with the charger?

Because it found someone else to connect with!

What did one flame say to the other?

We're a perfect match!

What did the bat say to his girlfriend?

You're fang-tastic!

Why don't you ever see Santa in the hospital?

Because he has private elf care!

What did the gingerbread man put on his bed?

A cookie sheet.

Why did Frosty go to summer school?

To brush up on his snowledge!

What do you call a group of musical whales?

An orca-stra!

Why did the man run around his bed?

Because he was trying to catch up on his sleep!

What do you call a bee that can't make up its mind?

A maybe!

What do reindeers say before telling a joke?

"This one will sleigh you!"

What's the snowman's favorite drink?

Ice tea.

What do you call a snowman who tells tall tales?

A snow-fibber.

What's a Christmas tree's least favorite month?

Sep-timber.

How does Santa stay fit?

He sleighs it at the gym.

What do elves learn in school?

The elf-abet.

How many bees do you need in a bee choir?

A humdred!

What do you call a classy ant?

Elegant!

What do you call a sick eagle?

Ill-eagle!

What fish only shines at night?

Starfish

What kind of dog chases anything red?

A bull dog!

What do cows like to dance to?

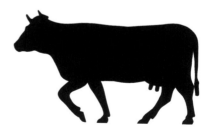

Any kind of moooosic you like!

Made in the USA
Middletown, DE
07 November 2024

64096755R00057